TINWHISTLE TUNES MADE EASY

by William Bay

MB22107

BIG NOTE/ LARGE PRINT EDITION

Visit us on the Web at www.melbay.com or billsmusicshelf.com

2   **Table of Contents**

Fingering Chart 3
Green Grow the Lilacs.....................................4
Tenting Tonight...5
Aloha Oe 6
Lament 7
The Foggy, Foggy Dew 8
The Ash Grove 9
Yellow Rose of Texas 10
Auld Lang Syne...11
Strawberry Roan 12
Johnny Has Gone for a Soldier 14
Ol' Dan Tucker 15
Blow Away the Morning Dew 16
Bell Bottom Trousers.....................................17
Old Shoe Boots & Leggins 18
Wait Til the Sun Shines Nellie 19
At a Georgia Camp Meeting 20
Marchin' to Glory 21
Goin' South 22
Oh, Sinner Man 23
Come & Go with Me to that Land 24
Bile' Dem Cabbage Down...................................25
Goober Peas 26
Captain Kidd 27
The Fish of the Sea 28
Jolly Old Roger 29
My Bonnie 30
The Bold Fisherman 31
High Barbaree 32
Greenland Fishery 33
Blow, Ye Winds 34
Cripple Creek..35
Sourwood Mountain 36
Big Rock Candy Mountain 37
The Roving Cowboy 38
When Jesus Wept..39
Blessed Quietness 40
There's a River of Life 41
When I Can Read My Title Clear 42
Praise the Savior 43
Great God When I Approach Thy Throne.....................44
Must Jesus Bear the Cross Alone 45
I am Bound for the Promised Land.........................46
When Jesus Left His Father's Throne 47
Jesus Calls Us 48
Lonesome Valley 49

The Galway Races...50
Cockles & Mussels 51
The Wild Rover 52
Love is Teasin' 53
The Galway Shawl...54
The Rose of Tralee 55
Brian O'Linn 56
Spancil Hill 57
Si Beag Si Mór 58
Bunclody 59
My Mary of the Curling Hair 60
Musetta's Waltz 61
Drink to Me Only with Thine Eyes.........................62
Southern Roses 63
Gypsy Theme..64
Hatikvoh 65
Santa Lucia 66
Do, Lord 67
I Need Thee Every Hour 68
Precious Memories 69
Mandy Lee..70
Daisy Bell 71
Up in a Balloon 72
Strike Up the Band 73
This Little Light of Mine................................74
Silver Threads Among the Gold 75
Grandfather's Clock......................................76
All God's Children Got Shoes.............................77
Little David Play on Your Harp...........................78
If You're Happy and You Know It..........................79
I've Got Peace Like a River 80
Bringing In the Sheaves..................................81
In the Pines 82
The Battle Cry of Freedom 83
Nine Hundred Miles 84
Down Where the Cotton Blossoms Grow 85
Christ Be Beside Me 86
Our Boys Will Shine Tonight 87
Columbia, the Gem of the Ocean 88
Mama Don't 'Low 90
She'll be Comin' Round the Mountain 91
Loch Lomond 92
Crawdad Song 93
The Mermaid 94
The Old Oaken Bucket 95
Doxology 96

Chromatic
Fingering Chart

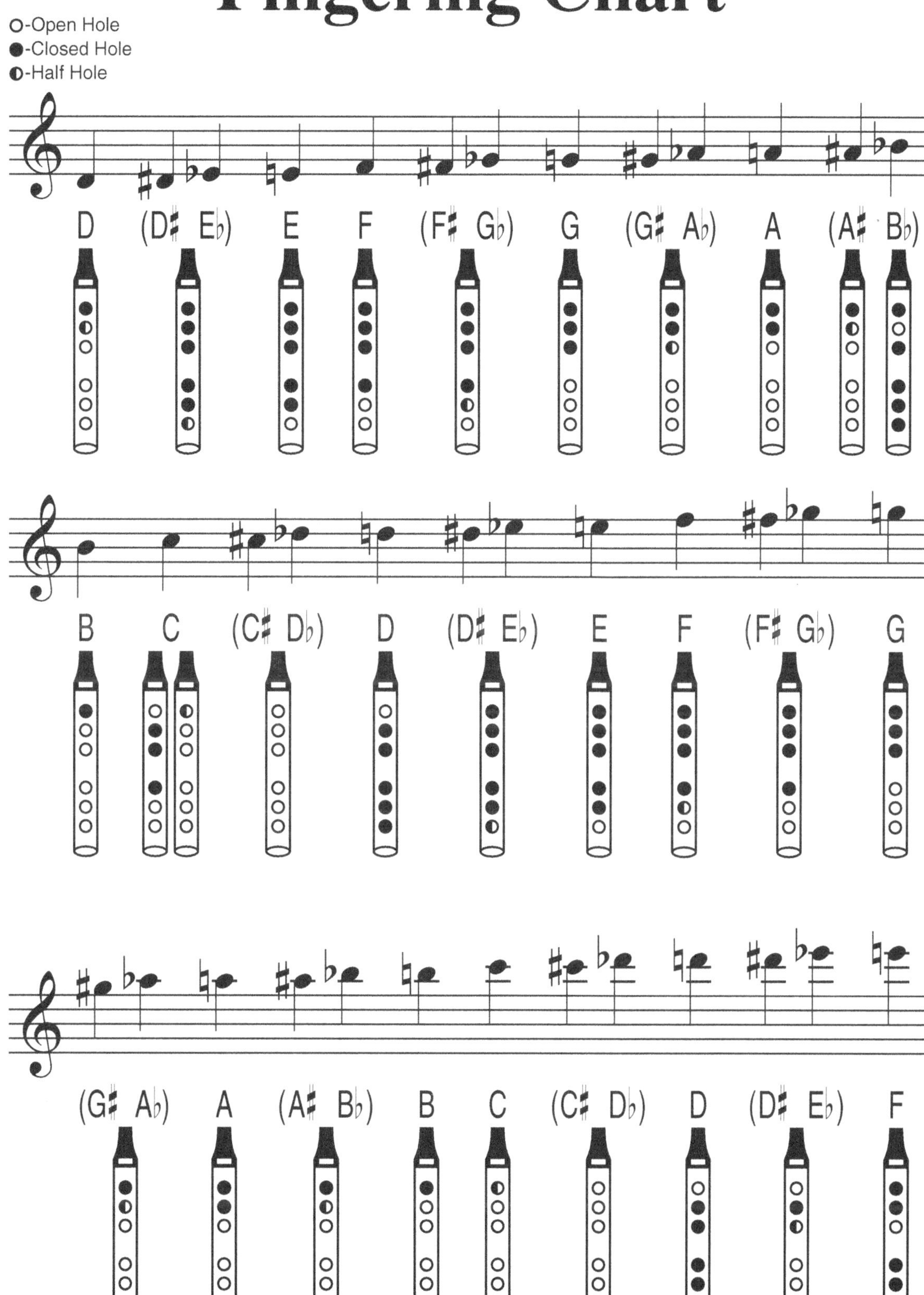

Green Grow the Lilacs

Tenting Tonight

Aloha Oe

Lament

The Foggy, Foggy Dew

The Ash Grove

Yellow Rose of Texas

Auld Lang Syne

Strawberry Roan

12

Johnny Has Gone for a Soldier

Ol' Dan Tucker

Blow Away the Morning Dew

Bell Bottom Trousers

Old Shoe Boots & Leggins

Wait Till the Sun Shines Nellie

At a Georgia Camp Meeting

Marchin' to Glory

Goin' South

Oh, Sinner Man

Come & Go with Me to that Land

Bile' Dem Cabbage Down ²⁵

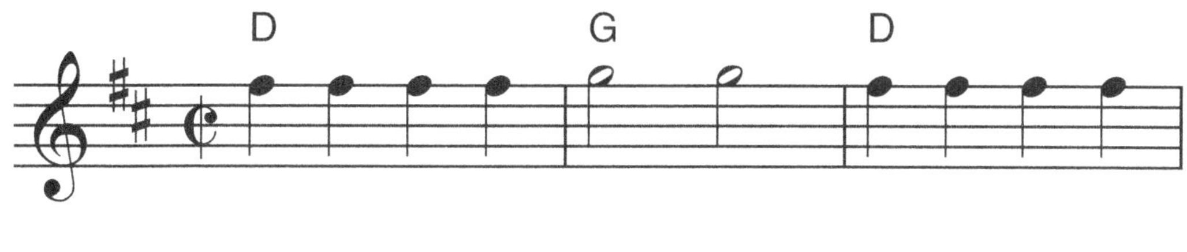

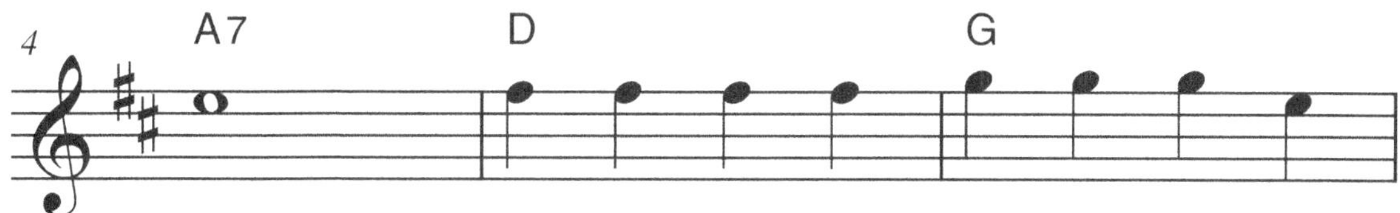

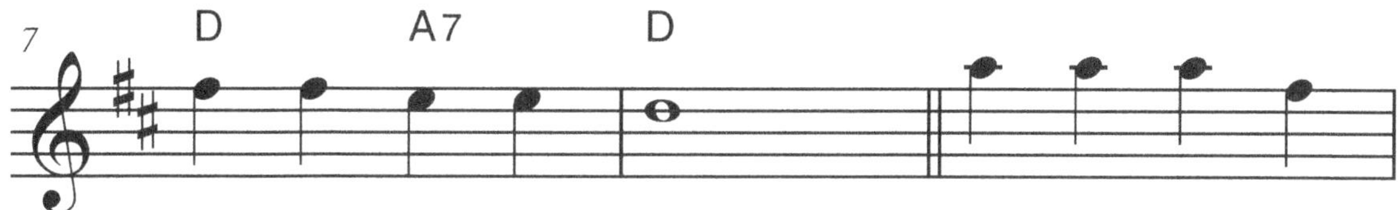

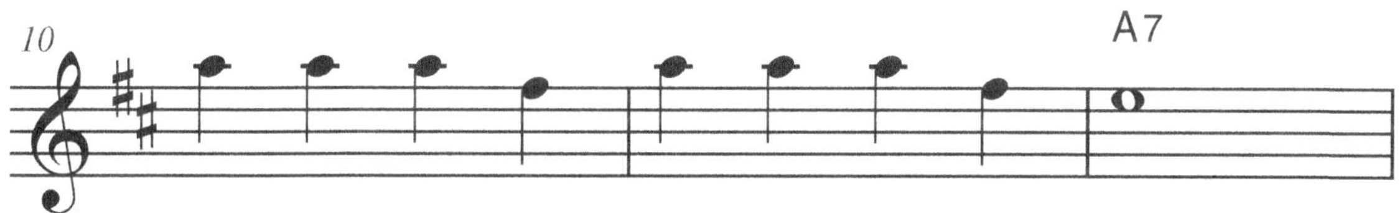

Goober Peas

Captain Kidd

The Fish of the Sea

Jolly Old Roger

My Bonnie

D
G
D
E7
A7
D
G
D
E7
A7
D
E7
A7
D
A7
D
E7
A7
D

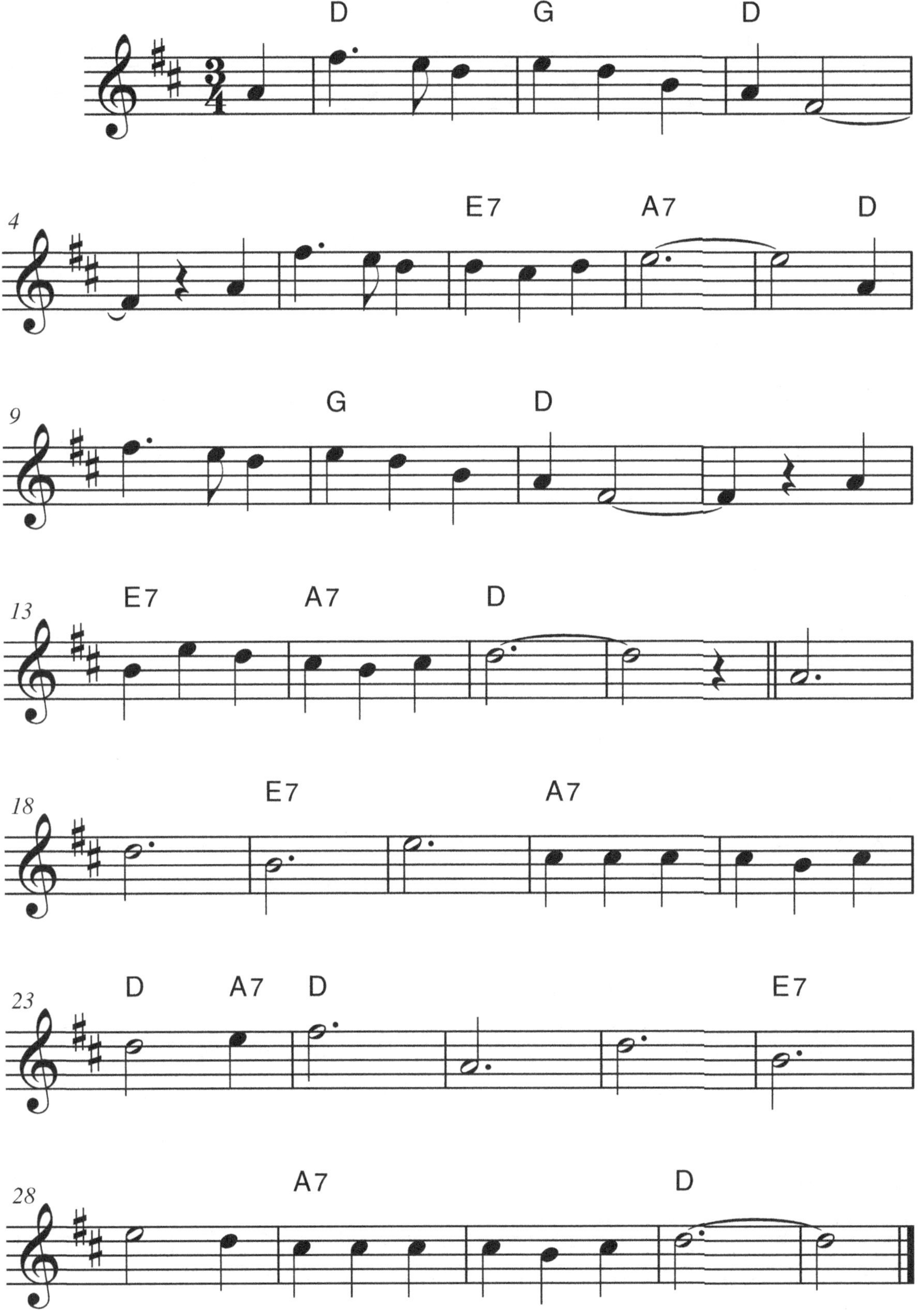

The Bold Fisherman

High Barbaree

Greenland Fishery

Blow, Ye Winds

Cripple Creek

Sourwood Mountain

36

Big Rock Candy Mountain

The Roving Cowboy

When Jesus Wept

Blessed Quietness

There's a River of Life

When I Can Read My Title Clear

Early American

Praise the Savior

Great God When I Approach Thy Throne

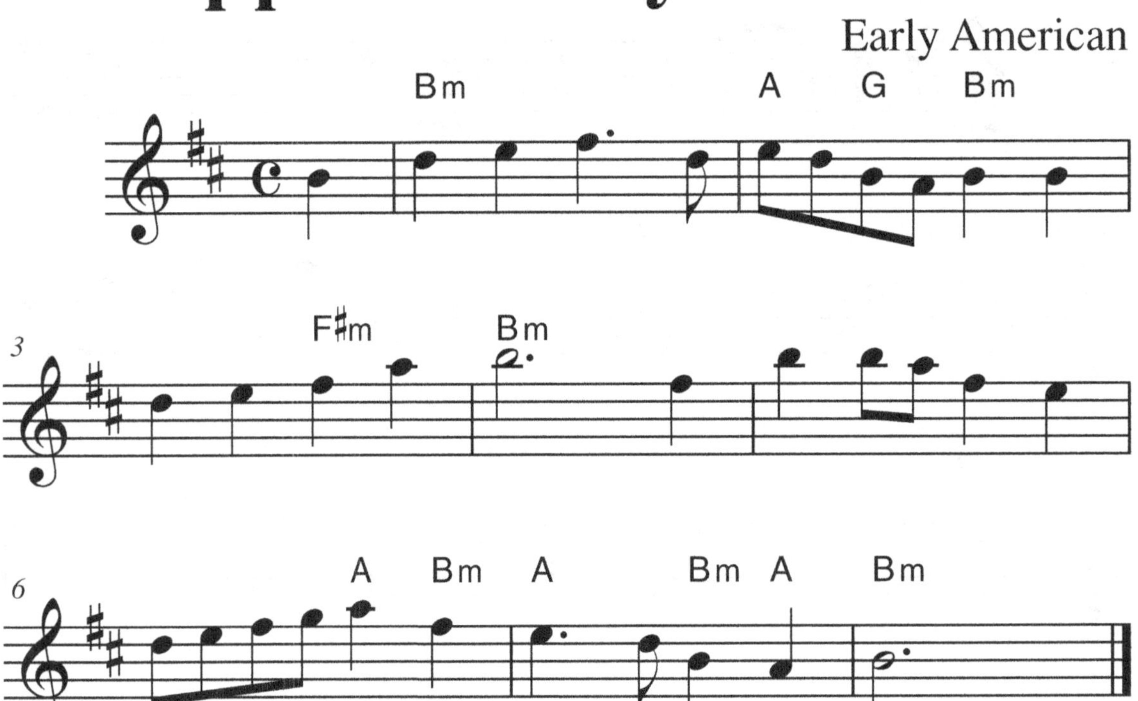

Must Jesus Bear The Cross Alone

I am Bound for the Promised Land

When Jesus Left His Father's Throne

Jesus Calls Us

Lonesome Valley

The Galway Races

Cockles & Mussels

The Wild Rover

Love is Teasin'

The Galway Shawl

The Rose of Tralee

Brain O'linn

Spancil Hill

Si Beag Si Mór

Bunclody

D
Bm
A7
D
A7
D
Em
D
A7
D
Em
D
A7
D
Bm
Em
D
A7
D

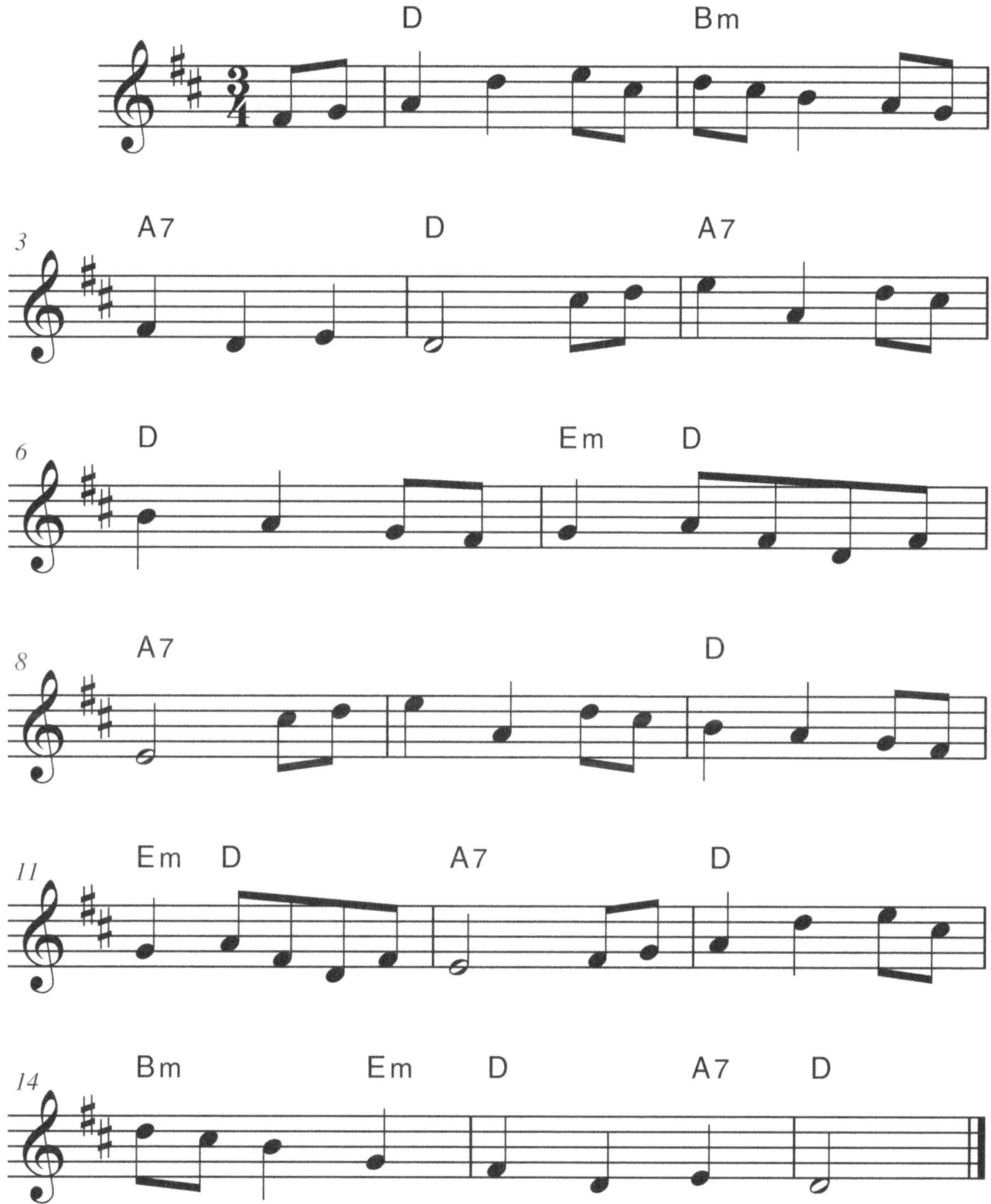

My Mary of the Curling Hair

Musetta's Waltz

62 Drink to Me Only with Thine Eyes

Southern Roses

Strauss

Gypsy Theme

Bm
Em
F#7
Bm
A.
D
Bm
Em F#7
Bm

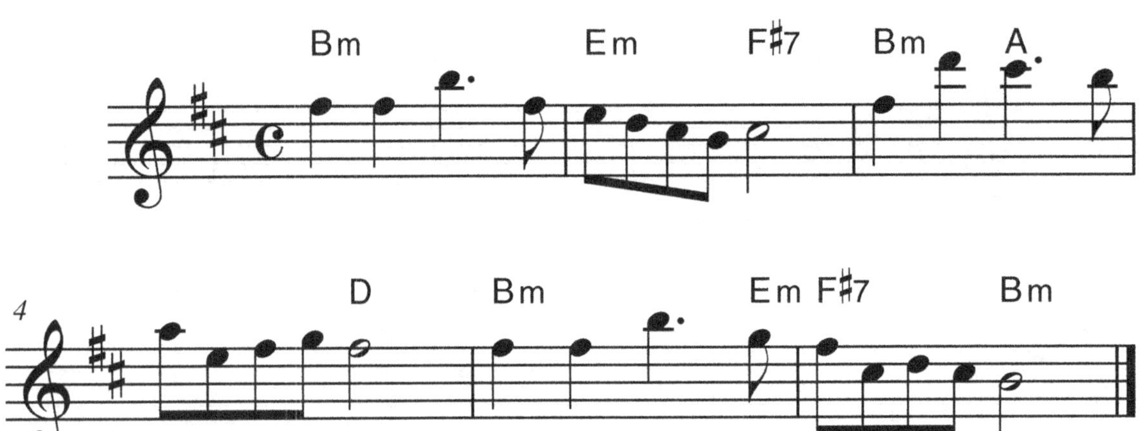

Hatikvoh

Israeli

Santa Lucia

Neopolitan Song

Do, Lord

D
D7
G
D
Bm
D
A7
D
D7
G
D
Bm
D
A7
D

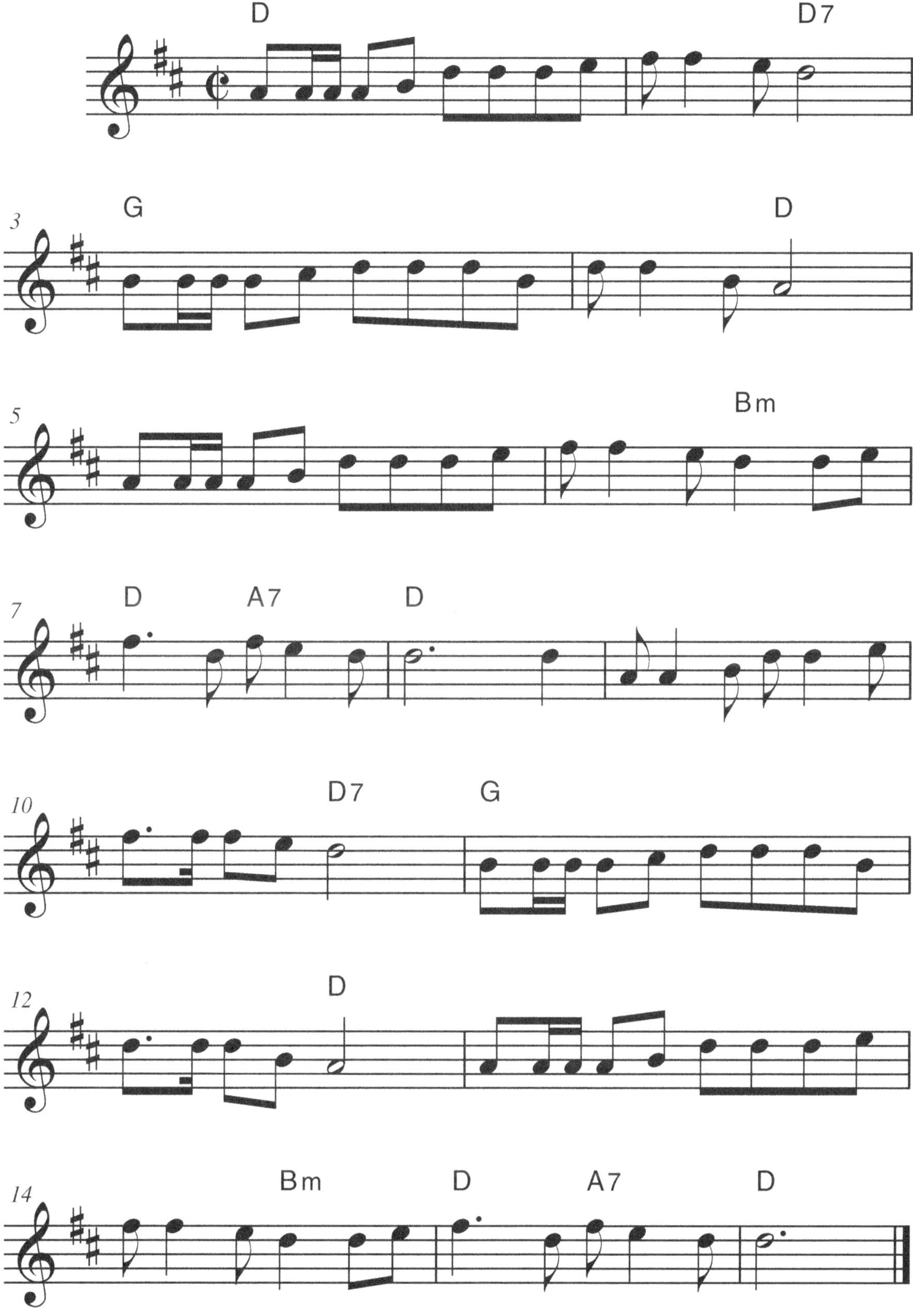

68 I Need Thee Every Hour

Gospel Song

Precious Memories

Gospel Song

Mandy Lee

70
Slowly
American Ballad
D   F#7   B7   E7
A7   G   A7
D   G   D   A7   D   F#7
B7   Em   D   A   G
D D7 G A   Bm Em D A7   D   A7   D

Daisy Bell

Up in a Balloon

Lively

Strike Up the Band

Lively March

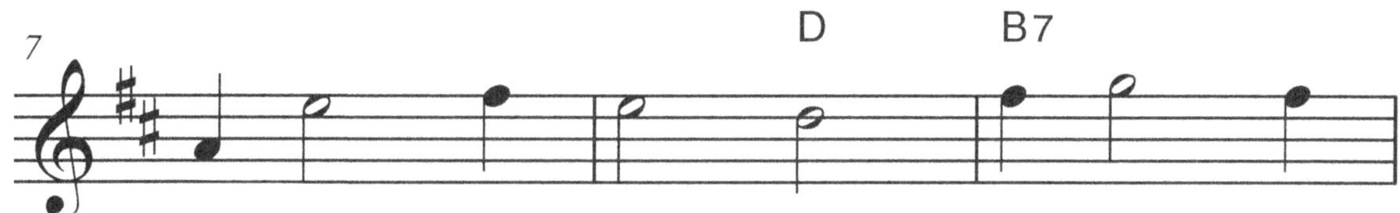

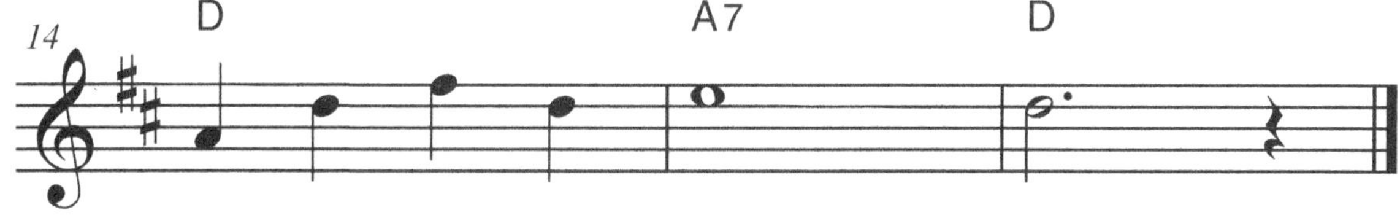

⁷⁴ This Little Light of Mine

Silver Threads Among the Gold

Grandfather's Clock

All God's Children Got Shoes

Little David Play on Your Harp

Spiritual

If You're Happy and You Know it

I've Got Peace Like a River

Spiritual

Bringing in the Sheaves   81

Gospel Song

D
G
D
A7
D
G
D
A7
D
G
D
1.
A7
2.
A7
D

In the Pines

The Battle Cry of Freedom

Nine Hundred Miles

Down Where the Cotton Blossoms Grow 85

Lively Tempo American Song

Christ Be Beside Me

Our Boys Will Shine Tonight

Columbia, the Gem of the Ocean

21
D
A7
G
23
Em
A7
D

Mama Don't 'Low

She'll be Comin' Round the Mountain

Loch Lomond

Crawdad Song

The Mermaid

Lively

American Sailing Song

94

The Old Oaken Bucket

Doxology

D   A   G   D   A7
D   A   Bm   Em   D
A7   D   A   D   A   Bm   G   A7
D   A7   D   A7   D

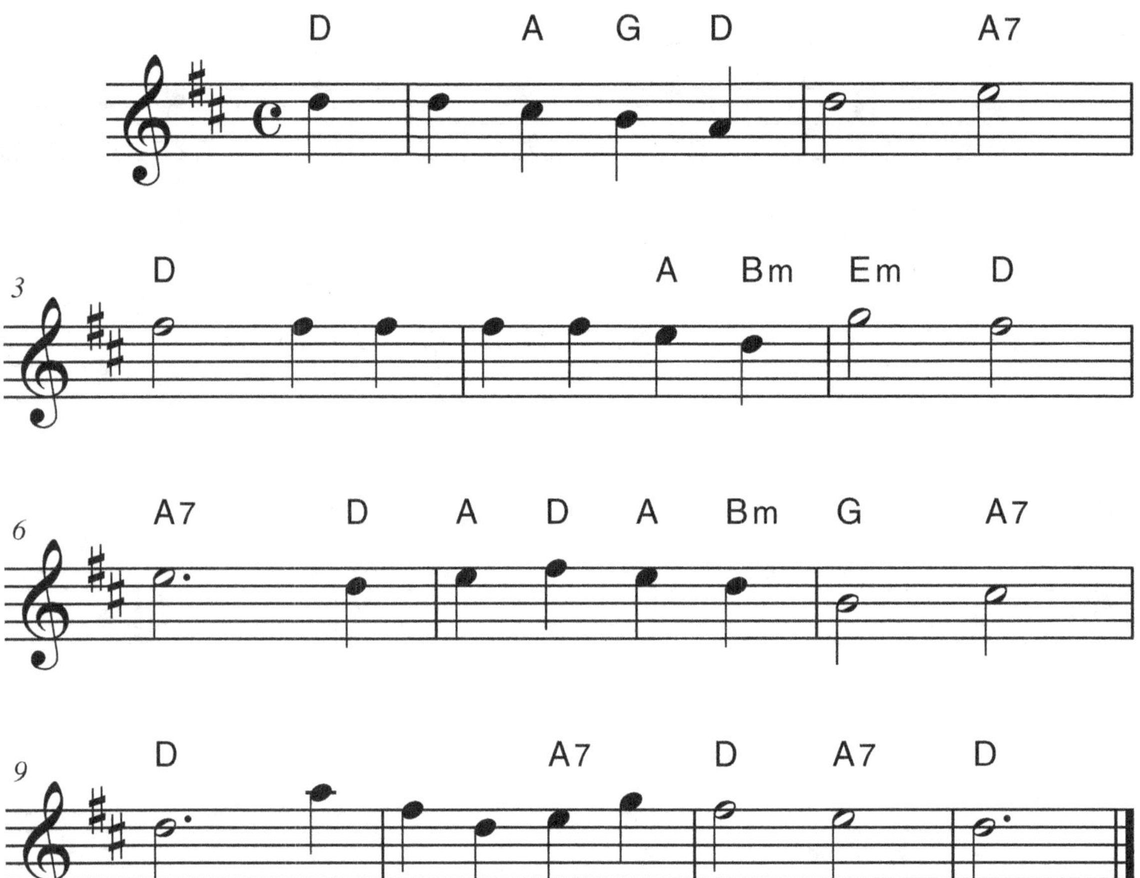

Made in the USA
Monee, IL
07 July 2026

56552249R00057